# The Poetry Of Everything From The Soul

### By Lord R.e. Taylor

# Dedication

I do hereby, by the power invested to me by the universe, dedicate this book of poetry to everything, everybody, and every place in our ever-expanding universe which inspires poets, artists, songwriters, authors, and actors to create such beauty in the world.

Copyright 2025 by Shadowlight Publishing
Ipswich, Queensland, Australia

ISBN: 978-1-7638437-1-4

## Poems For You

I have written over two thousand five hundred poems
Using many thousands of words
They were not written just about you
But every one of them was written for you
Some poems to make you think
Others written to make you cry
Still others, hopefully will make you laugh
The Lord knows I do not have much to offer
But I do know that my poems mean something to me
And I hope that they mean something for you

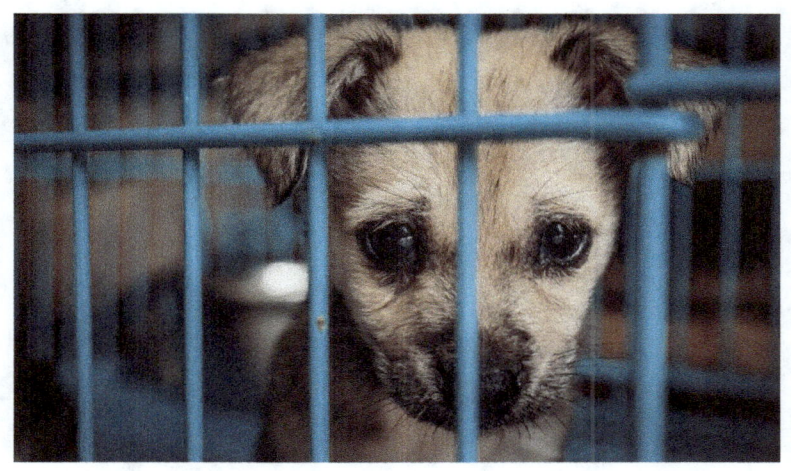

## Please Take Me Home

I know I am just a child
There is no reason for me to be here
I never barked or bit anyone
I just wanted to kiss you
And maybe play a little bit
Instead, I end up here
Watching people walk by me
Some look at me and smile
Others walk by and I never see them again
Please, if you can, stop and say hello
Maybe take me home with you if I touch your heart
I promise that my heart is already with you

## The Helpful Man

He was a unique kind of man
Always thinking about others
Helping any way he could
Even if it left him with nothing
No one ever hurt around him
But when the time came
When he was left with nothing
Not one person was there to help
No one even offered him a penny
They just turned their backs
But he was still a happy man
He did all that he could for everybody
And that was who he was
The only decent man he knew
And he was proud of that

## The Truth

No matter what you do or say
Twenty thousand years after you die
Your bones will tell the truth

## Take The Side Roads

My father always said
Take the straightest route
It is always the safest way to go
Trod by all sensible people
I found that yes, it may be safe
And well-trodden by everyone else
The most beautiful scenery
And the most interesting people
Are always on the side roads
Waiting for the people who are like them
Those special ones who take detours in life

## Windless

It may be scary
Out on a lake in a sailboat
And the wind just dies
Treasure that time of complete silence
The world will go on
And you could not care less

## Are We Alone?

Have you seen the world beyond
Do you think they have seen us
The universe is a magical place
It can be anything we want it to be
An endless, lifeless vacuum
A place filled with life
Maybe there will be some like us
Maybe some more advanced
Some may not be as smart as we are
It does not matter to the universe
Only your hopes of other lives matter
And the hope that someday we may be worthy
But if they are either friends or enemies
We will no longer be alone
And that will be worth celebrating

# Please Sir

Please Sir
I have very little left
No brothers or sisters
No mother or father
I live in the streets
All alone
I beg for food when I can
But food doesn't exist either
Please, Sir, I do have favor to ask
If you have even a single bomb left
Drop it on this innocent child
For I do not want to live any longer
Not in a world that does not exist

# Johnny Flowerseed

You must be someone new
Another Johnny Appleseed
Leaving flowers wherever you walk
So, please travel the world
Bring life and beauty wherever you go
And we will remember your name
Johnny Flowerseed

## The Small Shops We Remember

It seems like a very long time ago
Small shops lining the streets
In some cases, for blocks
Everyone was different
Offering anything you could want
Their people stayed with them for years
Not there one day and gone the next
These people were your friends
You knew their names and they knew yours
But that was a very long time ago
Before malls and superstores
For sure that was a better time
Friendlier and more caring
But it was taken away by money
And sadly, those small shops will never return

## The Magic Of Love

There are so many tales, all telling the same story
A prince awaits at the bottom of the stairs
Finally, the princess comes down one step at a time
It is always love at first sight and a happily ever after
So, after the stories are told thousands of times
The magic of the staircase still creates love whenever it can

## A Long-Lost Hero

When I was a kid, I loved picking apples
There was a tree standing on the top of a hill
It always had the best-tasting fruit
And we fought for the ones from the top
It was nearly two centuries old
Surviving so many blizzards and storms
Untouched by so much until last year
A gale came up from the lowlands
The leaves blocked out the sun for two days
Revealing a grave from so long ago
After that day when we went to gather apples
We thanked Captain Spencer Tate for his tree
And the apples we picked
A lasting tribute to a long-lost hero

## In Love With A Star

I spent so many nights alone
Looking from my bedroom window
There is always a star
Yellow, it twinkles in the dark
Resting on top of my gate
How could I not love it

## A Cassowary's Warning

How dare you come to my land
We never said that you were welcome
You just came and took over
Just as if you owned the place
Well, guess what…you don't
We are the Alphas here
We decide who comes and who stays
So, if you know what is good for you
Go back to where your kind came from
Or try staying in your cities
You might be safe there
But we haven't decided yet
Maybe we will let you know when we do
Maybe not though
That is all up to you

## Visiting The Bayou

There is a place
Everyone knows about
Although no one talks about it
So many strange things are there
Animals that would love to eat you
Witches and warlocks casting spells
And the living dead looking for you
Please, if you do not live in a bayou
Do not take the chance of visiting
So many people have gone in for the day
A lot of them never found their way out
No one knows what happened to them
Or if they do, they will not say
So, listen to the tall tales
Believe what those who escaped have to say
And stay out of the Louisiana swamps

## My Tears Flowed

I watched a family buried
My tears flowed
Not for the family
But for my mom
Who was buried nearby

## She Still Watches

She was born so long ago
Her mother left her after birth
Somehow, she survived
Lost away from the world
Without love or education
She was different from everyone else
Her world was silent
Only the animals to visit her
In all her sun rose and set on her
Some guess more than forty-five thousand times
But she kept to her life
Even to the extent of dying all alone
Still, her body sits in her favorite chair
Watching a door that never opens
But that was who this poor woman was
Unloved and unknown for her life
And now for her eternity

## Flowers For You

My love, I think you are a special woman
Please know one thing though
I will never get you store-bought flowers
You will never get a dozen red roses
Or any other flowers which are mass-produced
But you will get the best flowers there are
The flowers only nature can provide

## The Darkness

There is something great out there
Brought into traveling miles
Your journey will not be a usual one
A special time when your view changes
The world around you is gone
Hidden in the pure black shadows
There is nothing to see
Nothing to distract you
But there is always something there
So, maybe it is just you and your thoughts
Perhaps that is a good thing but maybe not
It is all up to you and the souls of the darkness

## Standing All Alone

You look so noble
Standing in the sun
But I do pity you
All alone with nothing around
Do you ever get lonesome
I feel like maybe you need someone
With no rain or snow
No shade from the heat
No paths to where you are
Do the birds ever come and see you
How could they ever find you
Even if they tried

## Cobblestone Streets

All around the world
There is art you can see
You can touch
And you can even walk on
Cobblestones are not new
They have been around forever
Still, very few take the time to look at them
The beautiful designs add
Other archaic haphazard designs
Each adds to the beauty of the medium
If you get the chance to walk a cobblestone street
Take time to look at the stones
Maybe touch a few
Their beauty may just make you smile

## Pushing You On The Swing

So many times, I pushed you on that swing
But that was during the warmth of summer
Now, our time is really limited
The days and months have passed too quickly
Winter's snows and cold are coming way too soon
But know I will be here to push you again when spring returns

## Love's Promise

He knows how important you are
His heart only beats when you are near
Dreams of you fill his sleep
And his daydreams show only you
He is proud of having you in his life
An integral part of a very long existence
All it took was for him to look into your eyes
And hear the first words you ever said
Love appeared in that moment
Promising to never leave
A promise it intends to keep

# The Lunch Counter

It was a whole other world
No cell phones or tablets
No text messages
People gathered and talked
The most popular places no longer exist
Every afternoon and all weekends
The place to be was the lunch counter
Woolworth's always had the best
Every store in every mall and street
Great food that never emptied your pocket
And a staff that would make your day happy
No matter what mood you were in
It is so sad that Woolworth's had to die
Sadder yet that the lunch counters went with them
But we do have memories and pictures
That way, they will always be alive

## The Ride

From the second of conception
Time begins its endless ride
Always traveling faster and faster
Leaving each breath behind
But we have no choice
We joined the ride before we knew better
Now, most of us are well beyond our prime
Still riding that ride
Collecting memories and feelings
Loving and losing the way the ride intended
We are hoping it will not end too soon
But also hoping it will end when the time is right
However, we do not have a choice
Whenever the conductor comes around
He will look carefully at our ticket
He will be the one to decide what station is ours
When he does that, it is when our ride ends
And he won't care as our ride leaves without us

## A King And A God

You were known long before white men landed
A legend that no one ever had the chance to see
You were both a king and a god
Watching over every creature of the forest
Yet you never asked for anything
It was just your love for those weaker than you
True, you may not exist except in stories
But the forests would not be the same without you
And that would be a shame

# A New Life

So many people pass by
Every morning and evening
Plain black asphalt for miles
No one looks away from their phones
They miss so much
Yes, it was a miracle
Only taking one day
A new life sprang into the world
Even with that no one looked
They just walked away
Never caring about anything
Yeah, it was just a flower
But it was life and it was beautiful
Too bad you didn't see it

# The Waiting Portal

Walking through the forest
You look and see a treasure
A portal to another reality
Just as beautiful as the one you are in
Do you dare take another step
Go through to the other side
Or stay where you feel safe
That, my friend, is up to you
The portal will be waiting for you
If you ever pass this way again

# Riding The Rails

Let's step back in time
Take a ride through a wonderland
Hear the clicks of the wheels
Feel the rocking of the cars
You can almost imagine the past
Cowboys and ladies traveling west
Building a new frontier
While trying to avoid masked bandits
As well as pissed-off Indian tribes
You never knew what was going to happen
But such was life back in our history
Whenever you went aboard a steam locomotive

## Seeing You

When I wake up my eyes are fuzzy
Unable to focus on anything
Except when I look at you
Your eyes, your smile, your everything
Maybe my heart takes control
And I see the perfection that you are
You are my life and my soul
I love you more than I ever thought possible
So, for now, I will gently kiss your lips
And let you sleep a little bit longer
Know that I will be here when you awaken

## Magic Of The Forest

The wilderness is such a beautiful place
A place where you can go and forget
It does not matter what you want to lose
Everything bad will be gone in just moments
Just listen to all of the spirits who live there
Their songs will lift you to places you have never seen
With serenity to calm every nerve
To make every dream a very pleasant one
They will even show you hope if it is lacking
Just go there for a minute, an hour, or even a day
So, take a chance and see what your new life would be
Yes the forest will do that and so much more for you
If you just give it a chance

## The Beauty Of A Flower

The beauty of a flower
Utter perfection
So common
Yet, it's truly hard to find
Most people walk by
Not taking a single look
While others will stop
Admiring the job nature has done
They will not pick them
Leaving them to make children
Babies that will continue their beauty
For many more generations to come

## A Chance To Live

We see that you are in pain
And we know that we may never understand
But please know that we will be here for you
So, know that you no longer have to hide
Showing us that you are always okay
Your bravery is not helping you
It is just going to make you worse and worse
Until the day comes which we do not want to see
The day comes when your heart beats its last
And you die at your own hand
So please curl up, cry, do whatever
Please, just give yourself a little hope
Maybe just enough to talk things over
Maybe just enough to allow you a chance to live

## A Proposal

There is a place
A most romantic place
Whenever I see it
I think of you
And I wish that we were there
I want to look into your eyes
Remember how much I love you
And ask you a most important question
I can only hope all those years
That they have not changed your feelings
Because I want to spend my days together
With you as my soulmate
So, I hope that your answer will be yes
When I ask you to marry me

## The Universe Is Yours

Sleep little one
The universe is there for you
You know that it is so close
Within reach of your dreams
So, as you grow keep your mind open
Always let your heart be free
And the universe will be yours

## A Shed On The Beach

It would be so great to be on an island
Find yourself a shed on the beach
It doesn't matter what it looks like
If it is all beat up....so what
It will have a character a new house wouldn't
Think about waking up right after dawn
Looking out from your bed
Seeing the peace of the palm trees
Hearing the sounds of the waves on the sand
And the calls of a hundred birds from the trees
All because you found a shed only feet from the beach

## Leave The Children Be

Children want to learn
They want to be creative
It is up to all of us
Their parents and everyone
Encourage those kids
Show them what to do
Then simply back away
Let them do it their way
If that means they make a mess
Just remember you did the same thing
Maybe even worse
Just hope that they never grow out of it
The world needs more creative people

# Missing The Snow

It is coming anytime
You do not want it
But it comes anyway
Think about it this way
Say you grew up with snow
You walked uphill to school in it
Snowmen grew to ten feet
And snowballs hit every inch of you
Now imagine you move to a place
Palm trees in every yard
And not a snowflake ever falls
Yeah, you can look at pictures
But it is not the same
You will miss the snow and the cold
And maybe even the snowballs
So, all you can do is remember
Sometimes perhaps watch a video
That will be the best you can do

## Then God Created The Bee

After God did His seven-day thing
He knew that He had something else
Something that He had to create
It had to be extremely cute
Maybe friendly to lesser creatures
Also, it had to be a great worker
All the life He created had to depend on it
So, He sat back and thought but it didn't Him long
He waved His hand and smiled
A bright orange and black bee flew from Heaven
On its first day, it found every flower God had created
And on that day life truly began on Earth

## The Peaceful Ocean

He never liked his life
Something was missing
He knew what he wanted to do
Just could not choose a way
But the waves looked so pleasant
Just swimming out into the sea
Relax and let the waves do what they do
No pain or blood
No way anyone could interfere
Just a few minutes drifting as he sank
Restful and quiet would be what he wanted
Then it would be all over
And he will find the peace he desired

## Be Proud

Be Proud
No matter what you do
No matter how you do it
It doesn't matter if you are good or not
All that matters is that you did it
And for that...you should be proud

## Your Light

I have missed you for so long
I know you are still out there
We may be an entire world apart
Still, I can see your light in the distance
It appears as a lantern in the night
Even at this distance, it is brighter than any star
Leading my heart back to you
Telling me that my love is not lost
Causing me to think that there may still be a chance
A chance for me to love you again
And we can share our lives again and forever

## Depressed And Anxious

There is something wrong with me
You cannot see it, but it is there
Sometimes it does get to be too much
It is not easy to face my life every day
Sometimes I must lock myself away
Depressed and anxious all the time
I was not like this a long time ago
But something went wrong with me
I do need someone to talk to sometimes
But only if I can find someone who understands
Someday, maybe I will

## An Unending Love

It is so hard to find love
Especially that special kind
Where they endlessly watch for you
Smiling and jumping up and down
Even before you reach the door
True, they don't have the ability to vocalize it
But Nature gave them so many other ways to say it
They smile all the time with their mouth or their eyes
Either way, you cannot help but smile back
They run and jump into our laps as soon as we sit
While they kiss every inch of our face
Having a friend like that is the best love you can have
That love will last for their entire life
And in our memories for ours

# A Green Christmas

Everyone wanted a white Christmas.
There was snow the week before
A lot of snow coating the ground
And gripping onto the pine needles
But on December twenty-third, things changed
The spirits in the South thought better
They sent tropical breezes our way
Every flake of snow melting
Leaving only tears on every needle
As well as in the eyes of everyone around
Yet, everyone celebrated their green Christmas
And they still had their "Merry Christmas"

# You Are My Eternity

I wish that minutes could be eternities
So the clocks could never tell us to part
Even for the briefest of instants
I have never told you this
This is my dream, my wish, and my prayer
You are the one I wish to spend eternity with
And that would make my life perfect

## Freedom?

Despite what they tell you
Freedom is never given
They will let you think you can use it
But they really don't want you to know
They can take it away at their whim
Not just for you but everyone in their country
You will not be able to argue the loss
Their troops will make sure you are silent
It has happened before, and it will again
That is something you know you don't want
And that is something that the world doesn't deserve

## Discovery

Take a walk deep into a forest
Don't ever follow a trail
That would be no fun
Instead, just walk wherever
The Fates will always control you
You may find something hiding
Something which may not be remembered
It may not have been seen in forever
But, lucky you, you have found it
You will see the beauty in its loneliness
Take time to look at it
Explore everything it has to offer
Please do not reveal where it hides
Let others share your thrill of discovery
And see the beauty that someone left behind

# 0's And 1's

Humans are at war
Trying simply to be
While tech takes over
If we lose our names will be gone
We will never feel another emotion
We will no longer become parents
Our lives will be lived on a computer screen
0's and 1's replacing everything and everyone
You, me and everybody else
Simply gone into the cloud
Never to be seen again

# I Love You

I never knew a woman like you
An immortal beauty
Blessed by the gods
A living sign of perfection
Yet here you are
Silent yet speaking so much
I have to say something
You have heard it so many times
Even though I do not know you
I do love you more than you will ever know

# Poppies

Four petals
Blood red
Saying goodbye
Honoring lost souls
Warriors killed
Long before their time

## The Long Road

The road looked so long
As if it had no end
But it had been travelled before
And it will be travelled again
All it would take is curiosity
The urge to do something
And the feeling that you are special
You know that first step is the hardest
Luckily the latter ones will be easier
The experiences will mystify you
Pulling you into your imagination
Your thoughts running wild
Changing your reality
And maybe your ideas about life
So, take the first step down that road
And see the person you can become

## Our Loss

Where is our history going
So much of it has been lost
Abandoned and left to rot
Or it is torn down
Just a vacant lot remains
Or a modern building
Steel and glass
Standing where a work of art stood
Built by people who do not care
And a loss to the people who do

## Twice A Day

Twice a day
Magic is created
Water leaves the shore
Leaving pools shining in the light
Allowing so many forms of life
Some seen for the first time
To experience the warmth of the sun
Their endless movements
Dancing between polished stones
Celebrating their lives in the sparkling water
They never realize they are prisoners
Still, they are happy when the water returns
And they can again swim in the endless sea

## Living For The Weekend

Forty hours at work
Doing the same thing
Over and over
You daydream a lot
You have to or you will go mad
Dreaming of being with your mates
Joking and sucking down some cigs
There may be some hot wings
Paradise on Earth
But one thing makes the wait bearable
Knowing that endless bottle of beer
Cold and tasty
They are waiting for you
Hopefully they will be enough to get you drunk
Maybe that drunk will last until your work starts
And you start daydreaming all over again
For a working man that is his life
Honestly, he loves the way his week works
After all, for him, it is his life
And that is just how he wants it

## The Last Centrefold

Honestly, I never asked for it
I really don't know if I want it
You cannot imagine what it is like
Twenty-four million people
All look to me to lead their country
I guess now I have to take the final step
I hope you like the sexy centrefold I did
Because it is the last one I am doing
So now it is back to the Outback
And what you could call my regular life
Besides that, I am sexier than that damn Quokka

## The Creation Of Time

Someone somewhere
Thought they had a good idea
Let's make a day twenty-four hours
So many in the daylight
Many more in the dark
No one had a say about it
Time was created to rule our lives
When do you eat or sleep
When do you have to go to work
But there was never enough time in a day
So, others changed the clock
Adding or deducting an hour a day
Still a day was not long enough
So, we sleep too much or not enough
Nerves become shot
And stress builds up beyond limits
But we have to deal with it
All because one man created time
And made us all suffer for it

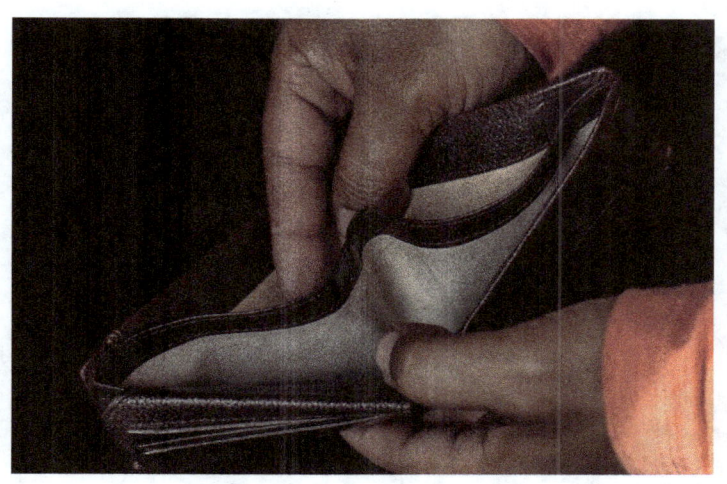

## Empty Wallet

I hope you never live through it
A big day is coming too quickly
There are so many people you love
So many gifts you have to buy
Yeah, your heart may be full
But your wallet is empty
It is very painful
You want to do so much
All you can do is tell them you love them
And maybe hope you see them smile
That will have to do at least for another year

## After The Storm

The storm passed
She waited until it was done
She looked through the window
Watching the rain and lightning
Checking the clock
She was more than patient
Knowing it was going to end
The moment it did
She became the little girl she was
Running outside, there was no music
Still, she danced and celebrated
A new day was here
And she wanted to live her way
Laughing and smiling the way she always did
That was what made her the little girl she was
She was happy again

## Shade Of The Shipyard

Praying to God is not going to help
She owns the Devil's Triangle
And she is out there looking for you
If you are unlucky enough to be found
The fires of Hell will not look so bad
As her spirit tears you and your ship apart
Just know that you will never be found
Your souls belong to her
The Shade Of The Shipyard will never let you go

## January Isn't January

I miss January back home
The ice and snow
The nip of an Arctic blast
I was home
Now January is not January for me
Green grass and birds chirping
Palm trees in the back yard
God, I miss home

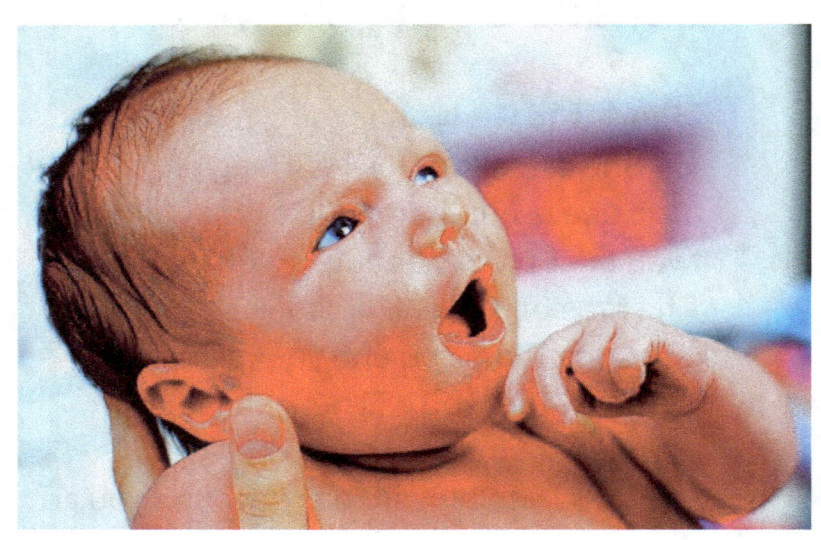

## Your Baby

Nine months is a very long time
From the day of conception
When a new life is created
The waiting begins
So does the hope and planning
All climaxing in hours of labor
When that little boy or girl comes
They burst into the world
Taking their first breath
Then they start crying their lungs out
But, when they open their eyes and look at you
At that moment stress becomes happiness
And your son or daughter becomes your life

## A Past I Never Had

I guess it wasn't my choice
But I was born way too late
I never had the chance to live my dream
Watching an old Black and white movie
While sitting in a movie palace with 2,000 others
All enjoying the best acting and stories
Directed by the best directors ever
Yes I can watch them on my 60-inch screen
But it will never be the same
The atmosphere just is not there any more
I guess things do change of time
Is it my fault that I miss the past
A past I never saw and never will

## Goodbye Charlie

When we grew up Charlie Brown was the man
But we never knew when Charlie, Lucy and Snoopy died
They just disappeared without a trace
Sadly, kids today will never know 'A Charlie Brown Christmas'
Their childhood will be damaged if not destroyed
All from the loss of a great American Christmas tradition

## Robin Redbreast

Sadly, winter is here
With the cold and snow
But you know it isn't going to last
The time is coming and not too far off
There are so many robins just waiting
And they know you are getting desperate
Soon they will all come to you
Winter will disappear and spring will come
All because a robin stops by to say hi

## An Angel's Tears

God's kingdom on Earth
No longer the paradise He wanted
It has fallen too far out of His control
Hate kills for no reason
And people celebrate it
Man-made diseases killed millions
And only a few cared anything about it
Maybe God does care in His own way
He would have sent His angels
Asking them to take the pain His people suffered
But they may only have so many tears
So, Humans have to suffer for things they have done
And they will continue to do so

## Snowflake

A child's life is special
Rushing outside on a winter day
Waiting with their tongue out
Hoping for that one, special snowflake
With the perfect shape and the perfect taste
That will make the child's day perfect

## I Will Always Love You

I cannot help it
I was born this way
Blame my parents
They made me who I am
Now you know what is going to happen
You are for sure going to love me
I will be your cuddly little furball
I just hope that your love will last
I will be here for ten years or more
But please remember one thing
No matter how old I get
I will always love you
And you will always be my family

## Country Road At Night

Traveling on a country road is best at night
You are all alone with your soul
There is very little of the world around you
Most of everything is hidden in the darkness
There are no sounds to be heard
And very little, if any, life to be seen
You really have no idea how far you have traveled
Nor do you have the foggiest idea where you are
You end up with an unknown amount of time spent
After all there is nothing to steal away your thoughts
True, you may not like it
But if you relax and enjoy the experience
It may be your best memory ever

## Eating A Chocolate Cookie

Are you sure you wanted to do what you did
I can imagine that she is a little angel
But you had a combination which would lead to trouble
Did you even look at the cookie before you gave it to her
A pretty little girl and a handful of semi-liquid chocolate
Did you think that anything else was going to happen
Maybe though you never gave the cookie to her
More than likely, she found the cookie jar and opened it
And suddenly three or four chocolate cookies disappeared
Now, if that was truly what happened don't you dare get mad at her
Just grab the one cookie left in the jar
Sit down with her and enjoy sharing her treasures
But Mom or Dad, make sure you make a mess eating it
After all, that little girl knew the right way to eat cookies
And maybe you could learn a little something about manners from her

## A Joke From The Fates

He only saw you for a short time
The Fates placed your cars together
It did not take long before you would meet
The two of you spoke the whole time
Then you gave him your name
Telling him to look for you and speak to you
His heart was beating so hard
It was not because of love but it was close
Now, he closely looks at every person he sees
Hoping that you will be walking past him
But that never happens
The Fates must be laughing out loud
Their joke worked and an innocent man was crushed

## My Best Friend

You are my best friend
I hope you know that
But I want to tell you something special
I love you and I always will

## A Joke From The Fates

He only saw you for a short time
The Fates placed your cars together
It did not take long before you would meet
The two of you spoke the whole time
Then you gave him your name
Telling him to look for you and speak to you
His heart was beating so hard
It was not because of love but it was close
Now, he closely looks at every person he sees
Hoping that you will be walking past him
But that never happened
The Fates must be laughing out loud
Their joke worked and an innocent man was crushed

## My New Friends

It was a warm, clear night
I saw my lucky star
My day was coming soon
So, we needed to have a chat
For some reason he didn't hear me
There were way too many stars
The heavens were there waiting for me
The night did not last as long as it should
When the Sun came up all the stars left
I was there all alone again
No, I never got an answer
But I did have a restful night
Just me and all my new friends

## Goddess Of The Darkness

You are the Goddess Of The Darkness
Blind to everything humans do
Still, you watch and you judge our actions
And protect those who worship you
Yet you choose the ones who will follow your partner
As she takes them down the long-lost trails
Crossing the River Styx to their final rest
But there is never any mourning
The living know that no harm will come to the dead
And that belief will keep them going
At least until you deem them ready

# We Love Our Dogs

We all love our dogs
They can be really smart
Doing thing we never expected
So many times, we say 'Oh my God'
But, c'mon tell the truth
Our dogs can be the dumbest around
Having trouble remembering their names
Much less any tricks we try to teach
Either way though we will love them
They will be our family forever
Just the way God intended

# Life

Life is a rare gift
Given when conception happens
We enjoy it while we can
Suffering through many pains
But it was never meant to last
When it is gone it is gone
So sad

# A Piece Of Art

There is art in everything
It can be beautiful
It can be ugly
It can be silly
Or it can make you say WTF
It can be on paper
On stretched out canvas
Or carved from a large stone
But it always comes from someone's heart
Even if someone tears up a sidewalk
Then lays down colorful stones
It comes from their heart
And it becomes a priceless piece of art
Something for everyone to look at and admire
All they have to do is look

## Her Winter Wonderland

She waited for almost a year
Went through the fresh green of spring
The heat of the three months of summer
And the beautiful colors of autumn
Dreaming of the moment the first snowflake falls
Her heart beats faster with every hour
Increasing with every inch of snow on the ground
Until the landscape is the purest virgin white
Only then can she finally smile
As she looks with pride at her winter wonderland

## Grown Up

You know Grandma
I always thought you were different from me
You know, kind of strait-laced
Prim and proper
I am so happy that you grew up
But you never really grew up
You decided to live life to its most
And be the real you
Kind of wild and free
Just the grown up you wanted to be

# The Power Of The Moon

As the moon rises in the east
Life settles in for a rest
But the life of the night rises
Screeching and howling
Flying in endless flights
Many souls leave their bodies
Leaving decaying corpses behind
Still, there is an apparent beauty
Cast by the shadows the moonlight creates
But it will only last so long
The power of the moon will be lost
And life will carry on just as before

## No One Will Listen

I try talking
But it never works
I speak the same language
Maybe a different dialect
But mostly the same words
I try and try again
It's always the same
If I ever have to talk again
I might try staying home
Maybe try talking to the kids
The wife or maybe even the dog
Ah, but they will not hear me
So, I will just talk to my mirror
At least then, I will have an audience of one
And I know he will at least hear me

# The Abandoned Church

How long have you been alone
People used to gather around you
Helping each other
Praying to their God
But their God walked away
The doors were locked
And the windows were nailed shut
All of the people left
Finding other places to worship
You were left all alone
To sit in a field and watch the world pass by
At least until you become just debris
And then everything will be all over

## An Oasis

From a distance
It is the most beautiful thing
An oasis created by God
Out in the middle of an empty sea of grass
A symbol of life abounding
With the chattering of birds
And the scurrying of the animal
It is a place to be left alone
Admired from a distance
But it should never be destroyed
Nor should it be bothered in any way
It is there for a reason
A reason neither you nor I can ever understand

## Take Time To Read

Human life is so hectic
Very little time to live
Much less try anything new
But there is something you can do
Open a book and start reading
It doesn't matter what kind
You can read as you listen to music
As you sit in a forested park
Or spend your time in the bath
Where you do it doesn't matter
Just enjoy the words in front of you
And let them take you wherever
Life will be waiting when you get back
I promise you that

## He Sits Alone

He sits alone
Crammed into a six foot by nine-foot cell
All he can do is think
He had happiness before
A wife who he thought was the most beautiful woman
He also had a daughter he may never see
They were the loves of his life
But that happiness is all gone
Taken away by the sound of a cell door locking
Now all he has are memories and dreams to keep him going
Well, those and the sounds of zydeco from a few cells away
But he hopes someday to be free even for a moment
Just long enough to hold his wife and daughter close
To make sure that they know that he has always loved them
And that he always will

## No To Death

You had your chance
The day he was born you touched him
You tried your best to take him
But even then he said no
So you have been following him
Walking behind him every second
Trying every chance to had
But he never spoke to you
Except to tell you to leave
He ain't ready and he never will be
So why can't you show some pride
Walk away and leave that man alone
Just go and never come back
You may be better off because you do

## America Is Back

You were always so proud
A leader in the world
Not afraid of anyone
And never backing down
For four years that all changed
Every country walked all over you
But you never fought back
You just hid and let them do it
While your leader hid under his desk
You became nothing
Now you have a new king
One who will not back down
Standing for everything that is right
He will fight for you and all of your people
That may make him hated by the ignorant
But most of your people wanted him
And they knew a good thing when they saw it
So, you may raise your head again
America is back!

## Mount Mee, Queensland

There is a little town
Barely a glitch on a map
Hidden away from the world
It is a beautiful place
With magnificent valleys
However, it is not a place to take a young lady
The name is far too suggestive
How could you ever ask a sweet girl
To go away for the day to Mount Mee

## The Beauty Of A Volcano

The scene is so pretty
Fire bursting out from the bowels of Hell
Dancing in the air to their own rhythm
Its smoke also reaches Heaven
Touching the home of God Himself
Pumice and obsidian spread for miles
Settling as a silent reminder as to events
While red-hot burning lava turns everything to ash
Destroying so very much but still saving history
Some towns have been preserved forever
All because a volcano erupted so long ago
And that is one we will always remember

## The Lost Hero

You were so famous at one time
Did so many fantastic things
Actually, you changed the world
Yet everyone ignored you
Giving credit to others
People who never did anything
You finally lost all your pride
Locking yourself into your room
You died sick and all alone
Even then the government harassed you
Stealing any evidence of your creations
Even so after long a time after you died
Everyone knows who you were and what you did
Nicola Tesla is who made the world what it is
And now he is the hero he should have always been

## The King Of The Forest

It takes so much
Performing everyday
Walking around
Sometimes playing with toys
Hoping someone would throw you a treat
You may have a friend or two
Other than that, you are alone
Just wandering around a concrete cell
You pretend to be happy
You may not know how your kind lives
But then again maybe you do
And in those few moments you do relax
It is possible that you dream
You may dream of forests and salmon fishing
You dream of hibernating through the winter months
And you dream of all of the cubs running around you
When you do I am sure that you will smile
That is who you were meant to be
The true king of the forest

# The Truth About Australia

Australia is so beautiful
Tropical forests go on forever
Plants not known anywhere else
Brightly colored flowers bloom
And grasses reach into the sky
So many animals, insects and birds
Life abounds in every meter
You must always be careful
Make sure you wear the right clothes
All Australians know the truth
Everything in Australia wants to kill you
So just stay locked in your car
You may be safe
But that is not guaranteed

## A Holy Miracle

It took seven days to make the world
Trees, animals, and birds of all kinds
Then two people who created us all
From that first moment our world was blessed
Now, an eternity later, we still have semi-paradise
A lot of the trees, animals, and birds have gone
But so many remain to make the world beautiful
Our Maker sees that we have loved His creation
Sometimes He will reward us in unexpected ways
Giving us a halo to show that we are still a holy miracle

## Grandma's White Velvet Palace

My finest memories were at my grandma's house
It was way far out in a forest that she loved
Summer, spring, and fall were beautiful
But, for me, winter was always the best
Only then was her house no longer just a house
It became her palace, surrounded by white velvet

## Outside The Window

Looking outside my window
A thousand people gather
Carrying signs and chanting
Protesting today's world
Are they right or wrong?
Who knows?

## Please Little Angel

Please little angel
You have done so much
Helping children in trouble
Taking them through their illnesses
Helping their dreams always be good
And when a child dies
You escort them to Heaven
So please, little angel
You, more than anyone
Earned the right to be at peace
You deserve the feeling it will bring
The feeling of being blessed

## For The Love Of Music

They have been around forever
Playing in taverns and fairs
On any street corner with people around
Usually, they earned a small pittance
A few cents here, a few more there
But they were always local celebs
Wandering minstrels faded away
And the music was lost
That was very long ago
The nice thing is that history repeats itself
Buskers replaced the minstrels
Again, they are playing in taverns and fairs
On any street corner with people around
Yes, they still only make a pittance
But they do it for the love of music
That is just the kind of people they are

## They DID Ask For It

There are some people out there
Maybe they can read, maybe not
If so, they need an intense talking to
They could be conspiracy theorists
Or perhaps they do not believe in sharks
Now, nobody should ever be hurt
But if they get a nip in their bums
You cannot say they didn't ask for it
Can you?

# Forever Love

My darling
Love of my life
I said that I would love you forever
That did not mean for as long as we live
No, my love,
When I said forever I meant that word
Forever is forever
It took me time to find you again
But I never gave up
My soul to me that you were out there
Maybe you were also looking for me
But now the Fates have brought us together
And I promise that we will always be together
Just the way we always should have been

# A Song For Her

He may be a superstar singer
And the best songwriter around
But there is one song he will never sing
She was his love for many years
Never apart for even an hour
Then, that summer morning came
He woke up and saw her lying with him
Her eyes were staring at him
And her mouth was in the most beautiful smile
He kissed her good morning
But she was no longer with him
He never got over the loss of his true love
He still remembers her with all his heart
So, he silently mourns by himself
Singing a song that only she will ever hear

## A Regular Guy

He may not look like much
Never seen in a suit and tie
He doesn't flash his money around
And he never looks down on others
He is just the kind of man you can share a beer with
And he knows his share of dirty jokes
He just wants to be a regular guy
And have good mates who just like him for him
We all know someone like him
Maybe he is our good friend
If we do, then we better appreciate him
Before, his kind don't exist anymore

## A Magpie's Thoughts

Please come out and sit down
I have something to tell you
You know, I am really not bad
Just do not do anything to me
I will leave you alone
If you do something to me
Chase me or throw rocks at me
I will remember your face
I will tell all my friends about you
And we will get you
So, just say "Hi" and wave to me
Only then can we be friends
Only then will you be able to walk safely
Believe me, it is all up to you

## A Rare Few Minutes

It only lasts a few minutes
That time when day and night meet
The brightness of the sun fades
And the blackness of night appears
There are some birds chirping in the trees
Cooler breezes swirl carrying sweet smells
And the streetlights cast a golden glow
As everything begins its nightly rest
A peaceful calm covers the world
For a few hours, the area can sleep
And renew itself for the next day

## A Poison Breath

I remember taking a breath
Smelling that sweet air
But now a mask covers my face
Removing poisons, they have released
I know never to remove it
Lest I become one of the bodies of the dead

## My Body And Me

Alas, my body is no longer mine
One after another, parts have failed
Turned their back on me as I aged
My bones and muscles went first
Making it hard to do the simplest things
My eyes will no longer be allowed to see
Both beauty and ugly now look the same
And the sounds of children fall on deaf ears
Many parts of me have been removed
Some, for even the simplest of reasons
Still, my brain works just a touch slower
Forgetting things, I wished to remember
But, despite it all, my heart still beats
So, for now, my life is still mine
And I fully intend to keep it that way

## A Child's Masterpiece

It may not be the Mona Lisa
But for children
It is their masterpiece
They should be encouraged
They could paint the NEXT Mona Lisa

## Heaven On Earth

So many people dream of a corner office
With an assistant outside of the door
And an intercom calling out to them all day
Instead, I always wanted a beautiful artist's studio
A place where my heart, mind, and soul could create
And I could find my Heaven on Earth

## Technology

When did we stop using words
We have used them for thousands of years
Then, the computer age arrived
Most of us still use words on them
But some spoke in pictures
Close to those of ancient Egypt
Now a new technology has arrived
Where words, numbers, and images no longer exist
Instead, everything is made of black-and-white squares
They are completely unreadable
That is, unless you use a machine to decode it
There is doubt that technology will stay the same
Since it has control of our language
It is frightening what may come
And they may use it against us
If there is any "us" left

## The Blessing From The Eighth Day

God created the world and everything
And He took just seven days to do it
But then he was tired and needed a break
He decided to spend a few millennia traveling
Checking out everything He had made
Walking was just dull, and camels were uncomfortable
So, He paused, raised His hands, and smiled
Before Him was a chariot of bright white metal
The chariot called to Him, and He answered
It was the only ride which was good enough for a god
But He did love the people of His new world
So, when He finished with His travels
He left a gift to His people with a new name
The Corvette became a symbol of God's love
And His blessing from the eighth day

## The Australian Blue Bee

I know that I am different
But I never did look good in yellow
I am in no way rare
Living all over this country
Yes, I do have a stinger
But I am not aggressive in the least
I guess I am a lover and not a fighter
So, if you see me flying around
Or if I ever land on your arm
Just know that I would never hurt you
I just want to say 'Hi' and maybe be your friend
So, just watch me and talk to me a little
I promise you that I will just fly away
Find me a flower and do what I was made to do

## Our Lost Eternity

When we are young
Time really means nothing
We have an eternity before us
And there is so much life left to live
Sadly, the years fly by
And our eternity begins to fade
Our remaining time passes too quickly
Just as if in the blink of an eye
We no longer have enough time
So, we do our best
Cramming years into mere instants
But always know that you lived well
And no matter how fast we lost eternity
There will be those left behind
And we will be remembered and loved

## A Child's World

A child cannot live in a gray world
It is against everything they believe
They will take that grayness and change it
Add not just any colors
The colors they choose have to be the best
The brightest and most beautiful they can find
With them, all grayness is erased
And their world is a more beautiful place

## The Way I Want It

All my life, I have lived in this world
Watching it change, but not for the better
So many are killing innocent people
Sadly, they are called the good guys
Governments work to make the world better
Their side is ignored and punished
While opponents call on their armies to attack
They only create hate and violence
But that is what they want
I do not want to be part of that any longer
So, I will find a place with no governments
And, happily, there will be no people
I will be all alone in my happy place
So, please do not try to find me
I will never come back
That is the way I want it to be
And that is the way that it will be

## Love Reborn

It is something everyone should know
A lot of people do see it as the truth
The best thing that any life can experience
Love can be genuinely universal
From person to person, it is happily shared
But from generation to generation
It can be taught from older to younger
That way, love will always be reborn
And hopefully it will become universal

## His Only Love

Lying in the dark, waiting
His mind thinks of you
The times you both spoke
When you walked in the rain
Remembering your first kiss
And the first time he said he loved you
But something bad happened
You had a life that you wanted
And he had a life that he wanted
Sadly, your lives were not together
Something had happened
Moving between you and driving you apart
Just you know that he does still love you
And he still wishes that life had kept you together
Please know that when the darkness comes
He lies silently and thinks of you
The only woman he had ever loved
And the only woman he will ever love

## Waiting For You

That clock has to be wrong
It says you have only been gone for a few minutes
But you have been gone for days or maybe weeks
Maybe you are never coming back
Then comes a familiar noise from the driveway
You did make it home, and we are happy

A Perfect Day

# A Perfect Day

It is the perfect time of day
No other person in sight
Calm breezes and silent trees
Just me and my best friend
Sharing our time together
Just as the Universe has deemed for us
We will walk together every day
And that makes every day a perfect day

## I Hate Mice

I know I am brave
As big as I am
Nothing can hurt me
I heard it
I never saw it
I knew it was there
I could not get away
I really hate mice

## Not Quite Such A Good Day

Today is going to be good
Not too hot or cold
No rain or snow
Could it be any better
I know I have stuff to do
A hell of a lot of stuff to do
But that hammock looks awfully good
Yeah, that and a big glass of beer
That could only make a good day better
I guess all that work can wait
Tomorrow ain't going to be so good
So, I will just do everything then
That is, unless the old lady catches me
Then today will be the perfect day to get everything done
At least that is what she says
And she is always right… ain't she

## The Paradise He Created

I felt His hand on my shoulder
He was giving me a chance I never wanted
Giving me all of His powers
He left me alone to think
Honestly, it did not take me long to decide
I saw what His children had created
I saw what His children had destroyed
And I knew what I had to do
I never said a word as I waved my hand
In that instant, all human life disappeared
Everything humans had created was turned to dust
And every single animal was allowed to thrive
Yes, I was God for just one day
But I made the Earth what it was meant to be
The paradise He created

This is the third book in the "Poetry of Everything" series, with plenty more to come. I sincerely hope that if you do get to read that, you will enjoy it as much as I did writing it

With all my love

Lord R.e. Taylor

www.ingramcontent.com/pod-product-compliance
Lightning Source LLC
Chambersburg PA
CBHW071906070526
44583CB00016B/1863